America Goes to War

The Revolutionary War

by Anne Todd

Consultant:
Melodie Andrews
Associate Professor of History
Minnesota State University, Mankato

CAPSTONE BOOKS
an imprint of Capstone Press
Mankato, Minnesota

Capstone Books are published by Capstone Press
151 Good Counsel Drive, P.O. Box 669, Mankato, Minnesota 56002
http://www.capstone-press.com

Library of Congress Cataloging-in-Publication Data

Todd, Anne.
    The Revolutionary War/by Anne Todd.
    p. cm.—(America goes to war)
    Includes bibliographical references and index.
    Summary: Describes the events leading up to the Revolutionary War, the life of
the soldiers, the major conflicts, and the outcome of the war.
    ISBN 0-7368-0584-2
    1. United States—History—Revolution, 1775–1783—Juvenile literature.
[1. United States—History—Revolution, 1775–1783.] I. Title. II. Series.

E208 .T63 2001
973.3—dc21   00-024312

Editorial Credits
Blake Hoena, editor; Timothy Halldin, cover designer and illustrator; Katy Kudela,
    photo researcher

Photo Credits
Archive Photos, 6, 9, 10, 17, 23, 26, 30, 34, 37, 39
North Wind Picture Archives, cover, 13, 14, 19, 21, 28, 32, 41

1 2 3 4 5 6 06 05 04 03 02 01

Table of Contents

Features

Dates of the War: On April 19, 1775, the Revolutionary War began with the Battles of Lexington and Concord. It ended on September 3, 1783.

Issues of the War: Many colonists opposed British taxes and the control Great Britain had on trade. They also wished to be able to govern themselves as an independent nation.

Battle Locations: Battles occurred throughout the 13 North American colonies. Some battles took place in Canada. Battles also occurred in the West Indies after France entered the war in 1778. These islands are located in the Caribbean Sea.

Major Battles: Battles of Lexington and Concord (April 1775); Battle of Bunker Hill (June 1775); Battle of Long Island (August 1776); Battle of Trenton (December 1776); Battle of Saratoga (October 1777); Battle of Monmouth (June 1778); Battle of Guilford (March 1781); Battle of Yorktown (October 1781)

Armies:

Continental: Early Continental forces consisted of state militias. These soldiers often were called minutemen. In 1775, the Continental Army was formed. George Washington commanded the army.

British: Great Britain had a well-trained army. Colonists often called these soldiers "redcoats" because of their red uniforms.

Important Leaders:

Continental: Samuel Adams; John Hancock; General George Washington; General Horatio Gates; Colonel William Prescott

British: King George III; General Thomas Gage; General William Howe; General Henry Clinton; Lord Charles Cornwallis

Weapons Used: Soldiers used cannons, muskets, rifles, and bayonets. Soldiers attached these metal blades to the ends of their muskets.

End of the War: U.S. and British leaders signed the Treaty of Paris on September 3, 1783.

Chapter 1

Before the War

In the 1600s, Great Britain established 13 colonies along the eastern coast of North America. The northern colonies were New Hampshire, Massachusetts, Rhode Island, and Connecticut. The middle colonies were New York, New Jersey, Pennsylvania, and Delaware. The southern colonies were Maryland, Virginia, North Carolina, South Carolina, and Georgia.

French and Indian War

By the 1750s, the population of the British colonies had grown. Colonists needed more land for farming and hunting.

France owned a large piece of land located west of the Appalachian Mountains. Some land west of the colonies also belonged to

King George III of England ruled over the 13 colonies.

various American Indian tribes. In 1754, Great Britain went to war with France and some tribes of American Indians over this land. This war was called the French and Indian War (1754–1763).

In 1763, Great Britain won the war. Colonists then began to move west. American Indians worried that they would lose land to the colonists. Several American Indian nations joined together under Chief Pontiac to fight the settlers. This war was called Pontiac's Rebellion.

King George III of England heard of the fighting. He then passed the Proclamation of 1763. This law stated that all settlers must return to the 13 colonies. No one was allowed to set up new settlements west of the Appalachian Mountains. Traders also needed the king's permission to enter the area. Many colonists did not agree with the king's decision.

Taxes

The French and Indian War was expensive. Great Britain had large bills to pay for the supplies it had used during the war. British leaders turned to the 13 colonies for help with these bills.

The British Parliament placed taxes on some items shipped from Great Britain to the colonies.

Great Britain won the French and Indian War.

Many colonists were angry that they were not consulted before Parliament imposed these taxes. The colonists felt that colonial lawmakers should decide what taxes the colonists had to pay.

The Stamp Act and Townshend Acts
In 1765, Parliament passed the Stamp Act. This law placed taxes on items such as legal papers and newspapers. Some colonists then refused to buy these British goods. A year later, Great Britain removed the tax because of the protest.

Several colonists were killed during the Boston Massacre.

In 1767, Parliament placed a tax on glass, paper, tea, and other everyday items. These laws were called the Townshend Acts. Again, the colonists boycotted these British goods in protest and refused to buy the taxed items.

Many colonists became angry with the British government because of these taxes. On March 5, 1770, a group of colonists began to throw snowballs and rocks at British soldiers in Boston. The soldiers fired their weapons into the crowd. Five colonists were killed and several wounded.

This event was called the Boston Massacre. Parliament decided to remove all taxes on the colonies except for the tea tax.

Boston Tea Party

Some colonists wanted to take action against Great Britain. One such person was Samuel Adams of Boston.

In 1773, Adams helped organize the tea merchants. They wanted to make sure that tea arriving on British ships was not unloaded. The colonists then would not have to pay any tea taxes to Great Britain.

On December 16, 1773, a group of Boston colonists climbed aboard a British ship. This ship carried a large tea shipment. The colonists did not want the British to know who they were. They disguised themselves as American Indians. The colonists then dumped the tea overboard. This protest was called the Boston Tea Party.

The Boston Tea Party angered members of the British Parliament. In 1774, they then passed what colonists called the Intolerable Acts. These laws prevented all trade in Boston's port. They made it illegal for colonists to have town meetings. Parliament also passed the Quartering Act in

1774. This law forced colonists to allow British soldiers to stay in their homes.

Great Britain sent more soldiers to the colonies. These soldiers were under the command of General Thomas Gage. The soldiers' bright red coats constantly reminded the colonists of British rule.

Colonists Divided

The colonists had different feelings about the British. About one-quarter of the colonists wanted to remain loyal to Great Britain. These colonists were called loyalists.

About a third of the colonists did not want to pay any of Great Britain's taxes. They wanted to form an independent nation. These colonists were called patriots. A small group of patriots called themselves the Sons of Liberty. They openly protested Great Britain's rule over the colonies.

Nearly half of the colonists did not want to take sides. They wanted to remain neutral in the conflict between the British and the patriots. But they were forced to choose sides once the war began.

British troops enforced Parliament's laws in the colonies.

Chapter 2

A Call to Arms

In September 1774, a group of colonial leaders met at Carpenters' Hall in Philadelphia. They formed the First Continental Congress. These men wrote a Declaration of Rights for the colonies. This document stated that the colonies did not accept British taxes. It also stated that the colonists agreed not to buy British goods. The Continental Congress then sent the Declaration of Rights to King George III. He refused to accept it.

Preparing for War

Patriot leaders such as Samuel Adams, John Hancock, and Patrick Henry prepared to fight for their freedom. They organized a group of soldiers called minutemen. Minutemen agreed

Minutemen were prepared to fight at a minute's notice.

to gather at a minute's notice to fight. Minutemen also were called the Sons of Liberty.

The Daughters of Liberty also helped protest British rule. This group of women made clothes for soldiers and boycotted British goods.

Minutemen began to store weapons in the town of Concord, Massachusetts. General Gage then sent soldiers to Concord to take these weapons. The soldiers also had orders to capture Samuel Adams and John Hancock.

Patriots Paul Revere, William Dawes, and Samuel Prescott went to warn people in Concord of the British plans. Revere and Dawes made it to Lexington. This town is near Concord. They warned Adams and Hancock. But British troops captured Revere before he could reach Concord. The British troops forced Dawes to return to Lexington before he could reach Concord.

Prescott continued on to Concord. He warned colonists there that British soldiers were coming. As a result, minutemen rushed to meet the British at Lexington.

Battles of Lexington and Concord

About 600 British soldiers marched from Boston to Lexington on April 19, 1775. British Major

Paul Revere rode to warn the colonists that the British were coming.

Pitcairn led them. They found Captain John Parker and 70 minutemen waiting.

It is not known who fired the battle's first shot. But it became known as "the shot heard around the world." It also signaled the start of the Revolutionary War.

The minutemen were outnumbered and lost the battle at Lexington. The British troops then marched toward Concord. But about 500 minutemen met them as they approached the bridge into Concord. Another battle took place.

Word of this battle spread quickly. More minutemen joined the fighting. They forced the British troops to retreat back to Boston. Many British soldiers were wounded or killed.

The Continental Army

On May 10, 1775, the Second Continental Congress met in Philadelphia. Members elected John Hancock as their president. They decided to organize an army. At the time, Congress needed to rely on volunteers. Congress did not have the power to conduct a draft to force colonists to serve in its army. Congress members selected George Washington to lead the Continental Army.

King George III was not worried about the Continental Army. He had a large, well-trained army. But these troops soon discovered that British fighting methods did not always work in the colonies. Revolutionary War battles did not always take place on large, open battlefields as they did in Europe. Some British soldiers also were reluctant to fight against colonists. Many colonists originally were from Great Britain.

British military leaders were forced to find additional troops. They hired Hessian soldiers from what is now Germany.

Minutemen gathered to force the British to retreat at the Battle of Concord.

Enlistment in the Continental Army

The Continental Army was inexperienced in warfare. Most of the soldiers were farmers. But they were eager to fight for their freedom.

By July 1775, about 17,000 men had joined the Continental Army. But they only joined the army for a year of service or less. Washington struggled to keep the soldiers from leaving the army when their term of service was over. By December, less than 6,000 men still were enlisted in the army.

Washington had to depend on militiamen and Continental soldiers to make up his army. Militiamen only enlisted in the army for a few months at a time. They had farms to run and could not commit to long periods of time away from home.

Women were not allowed to fight in the war. Most women stayed home with their children and worked on their farms. But a few disguised themselves as men and fought. Some women also followed the soldiers as they marched between battles. These camp followers often were the wives or mothers of soldiers. They cooked and did laundry for the soldiers. They also cared for the wounded.

Most American Indians did not want to fight in the war. A few fought alongside the patriots. But most sided with the British. They hoped Great Britain would help stop the colonists' westward expansion.

Uniforms

Uniforms for the colonists were in short supply. Soldiers usually wore hunting shirts. Few soldiers were fortunate enough to receive a uniform.

Soldiers in the Continental Army wore blue coats with white pants.

The Continental Army did not have one color of uniform to represent it until October 1779. At this time, Washington ordered all Continental Army coats changed to blue. The coat's collar, cuffs, and trim were different colors depending on a soldier's region. For example, soldiers from the New England colonies wore uniforms with a white collar, cuffs, and trim.

Soldiers often had no shoes. In the winter, shoeless soldiers wrapped their feet in cloth.

Weapons and Training

Training troops was difficult. Washington did not have experience leading a large army. He also had many inexperienced soldiers with short enlistment times. Washington constantly had new, untrained soldiers in his army. This fact made it difficult for him to teach soldiers in his army standard fighting methods.

Washington instead trained his soldiers to perform hit-and-run attacks. At the time, muskets were very inaccurate. Soldiers had difficulty hitting distant targets with them. Armies waited until they were near each other to fire their weapons. After firing muskets, armies charged toward each other with bayonets. Washington instructed his soldiers to quickly retreat after attacking with these metal blades. They then had time to reload their weapons.

The Continental Army used various weapons on the battlefield. Muskets were the most common weapon. But Continental soldiers also used rifles. These guns took longer to load than muskets. But they were more accurate at greater distances. Soldiers used tomahawks as camp tools. But soldiers sometimes used these axes in battle. The Continental Army also used cannons.

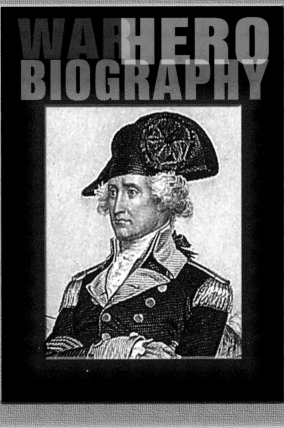

George Washington (1732–1799)

Washington was born February 22, 1732, in a small farmhouse near the Potomac River in Virginia. In 1754, he fought for the British in the French and Indian War (1754–1763). In 1755, he was placed in charge of the army in Virginia because of his bravery during the war. In 1759, he retired from the army and married Martha Custis. Washington attended the first Continental Congress in 1774. In 1775, he was elected commander of the Continental Army at the second Continental Congress. In 1789, he was elected as the first president of the United States. He was elected again in 1793. He died on December 14, 1799.

Saratoga

Bunker Hill

Concord

Lexington   Boston

Trenton

Valley Forge

Philadelphia   Monmouth

Yorktown   Chesapeake Bay

Guilford Courthouse

King's Mountain

Camden

Charleston

N
W   E
S

Chapter 3

Major Battles

The Revolutionary War included many small battles. Soldiers most often fought whenever they came across each other. But a few major battles helped determine the outcome of the war.

Battle of Bunker Hill

On June 17, 1775, minutemen fought the Battle of Bunker Hill near Boston. Most of the fighting actually took place on Breed's Hill. William Prescott commanded the colonial forces.

General William Howe commanded the British troops. He ordered troops up Breed's Hill. The minutemen repeatedly pushed the British soldiers back. But the patriots ran out of gunpowder after several hours. The British then charged with bayonets. The patriots fled and the

Washington's army was forced to retreat at the Battle of Long Island.

British captured the hill. But about 50 percent of the British soldiers were injured or killed during the battle.

Victory and the Declaration of Independence

Washington and his newly assembled army won its first victory at Dorchester Heights. On March 4, 1776, Washington's troops gathered on these hills overlooking the Boston Harbor. They fired their cannons at the British troops.

The British retreated to ships docked in the Boston port and left.

Also in 1776, the colonies officially declared their independence from Great Britain. Patriot leader Thomas Jefferson wrote the Declaration of Independence. Congress approved it on July 4, 1776. The 13 colonies then considered themselves to be free states.

Battles of Long Island and Trenton

In August 1776, British General Howe and his soldiers fought the Continental Army in the Battle of Long Island. Howe's soldiers also captured thousands of patriots. Washington's troops were forced to retreat.

After several more defeats, Washington led a surprise attack on the morning of December 26, 1776. He and his troops marched through a snowstorm toward Trenton, New Jersey. His soldiers were tired, hungry, and poorly clothed. But they still followed Washington across the Delaware River. A group of Hessian soldiers were asleep on the other side of the river. After a brief battle, the patriots captured nearly 900 Hessian soldiers.

The Continental Army forced the British to surrender at the Battle of Saratoga.

Enlistments increased after the Battle of Trenton. Washington also hoped to convince soldiers to stay in the army. He offered $10 to any soldier who would stay an additional 6 weeks. Many soldiers agreed to his terms.

Battle of Saratoga
In October 1777, British General John Burgoyne faced Colonial General Horatio Gates at the Battle of Saratoga. The British

planned to take control of the Hudson River in New York. Burgoyne attacked Continental forces. But Gates' soldiers pushed back the British troops. Burgoyne eventually surrendered his entire army of 5,700 men.

This victory helped patriot leader Benjamin Franklin convince France that the patriots could win the war. In February 1778, France agreed to help the patriots fight the British. French leaders hoped to gain back land lost to Great Britain during the French and Indian War. Later, Spain and the Netherlands joined forces with France against Great Britain.

Chapter 4

Life in Camp

Camp life for Continental soldiers was difficult. They had little food and clothing. They often were tired from battles and marching. Many soldiers lived without blankets or shoes.

Food and Lodging

Between battles, soldiers set up temporary camps. The soldiers divided into groups of five or six. These soldiers were messmates. They cooked, ate, and slept in the same tents or huts together.

Soldiers' rations consisted of meat and flour. The flour was mixed with water to make a flat bread. Soldiers sometimes found wild, fresh fruit. They also took food such as carrots or potatoes from fields. Water often was unsafe to drink. Instead, soldiers drank rum, beer, or tea.

Soldiers lived in temporary camps between battles.

Medical care was scarce for wounded soldiers.

Soldiers built more permanent camps to live in during the winter. These camps included a hospital, a building to store ammunition, and a building for food rations. They also included soldiers' living quarters.

Women performed many duties for the soldiers in camps. They ran slaughter houses that were located about 1 mile (1.6 kilometers) from the camps. Here, they killed animals such as cows and prepared the meat for soldiers. Women also cooked and did laundry for the soldiers.

Diseases

Diseases were a problem in the camps. Before the war, people from the 13 colonies had little contact with each other. During the war, diseases from different areas quickly spread as colonists mixed together. Smallpox and measles were common throughout the camps. Spoiled food and unclean conditions also led to the spread of diseases.

Medical treatment and medicine were scarce during the Revolutionary War. More soldiers died from diseases than died in battle.

Free Time

Soldiers worked and trained hard in camps. But they did have some free time.

During free time, soldiers read books. They spent much time praying and attending religious services. Some soldiers enjoyed carving wood. They often created useful items such as cups or gunpowder measurers. Soldiers played games such as backgammon and darts. Soldiers wrote letters home. They also hunted and fished to pass the time and provide food.

Chapter 5

Final Battles

Continental soldiers spent the winter of 1777 and 1778 at Valley Forge, Pennsylvania. This winter was difficult for the troops. Soldiers were poorly clothed and lacked food. Many soldiers died. Others deserted the army.

Baron Friedrich von Steuben of Prussia joined the troops that winter. Steuben supported the colonists' fight for independence. He also was an excellent military instructor. He trained the soldiers and taught them important military skills. By winter's end, Washington's troops were well prepared to continue fighting.

Battle of Monmouth

In June 1778, General Henry Clinton led the British Army at the Battle of Monmouth, New

Washington and his Continental soldiers spent a difficult winter at Valley Forge.

Jersey. General Charles Lee led the colonial troops. After the battle began, Lee suddenly ordered his troops to retreat.

Washington was angry at Lee's orders. He rode into battle himself and took charge of the colonial forces. During the night, the British retreated and the Continental Army won the battle. The skills the soldiers learned at Valley Forge had paid off.

John Paul Jones

The Continental Army did not own many ships. This meant that the British Navy could easily transport troops and supplies along the Atlantic coast. Colonial forces had to march over land. This took longer than traveling by ships.

In 1778, John Paul Jones raided British supply ships. He stole supplies and equipment for the patriots.

In September 1779, Jones's ship *Bonhomme Richard* battled the British ship *Serapis*. This battle took place near Great Britain's coast. Jones's ship was badly damaged in the battle.

John Paul Jones captured the British ship *Serapis*.

He ordered his sailors to tie their ship to the *Serapis* and keep fighting. The *Bonhomme Richard* sank. But Jones captured the *Serapis* and sailed away on it.

Battles in the South

After 1779, battles began to take place in the southern colonies. The British won most of these battles. British troops took control of Georgia in 1779. In 1780, they attacked Charleston, South Carolina, and captured more than 5,000 colonial prisoners.

In August 1780, British and colonial forces met at Camden, South Carolina. Lord Cornwallis led the British troops and General Gates led colonial forces. But many of Gates' soldiers were sick and starving. They fled when the battle began. Gates also fled the battle site.

General Nathanael Greene replaced Gates. Like Washington, Greene practiced hit-and-run fighting methods.

In March 1781, Greene led his troops against Cornwallis at the Battle of Guilford Courthouse near Greensboro, North Carolina. Cornwallis forced Greene to retreat. But many British soldiers were killed or wounded in the fighting.

Greene's forces fought the British in several small battles throughout the South. His troops won many of these battles. By the fall of 1781, British forces had retreated either to Charleston, South Carolina, or Savannah, Georgia. The Continental Army then controlled the rest of the South.

Loyalists

Not all colonists supported the war. Many remained loyal to Great Britain. Others were tired of the war and wanted it to end.

Patriot forces defeated Loyalist forces at the Battle of King's Mountain.

The Declaration of Independence made it illegal to support Great Britain. Nearly 80,000 people left the colonies after the declaration was approved by Congress. But many people in the south decided to fight against the patriots.

In October 1780, loyalist and patriot forces fought at the Battle of King's Mountain in South Carolina. The patriots killed 150 loyalists and captured 600 others. This battle helped end loyalist support. British supporters were afraid to join loyalist forces after the patriots' victory.

Ending the Revolutionary War
The war's final battle took place in 1781 at Yorktown, Virginia. This town was a river port on the Chesapeake Bay. Cornwallis brought an army of 7,000 there to wait for supplies.

Washington learned that a French fleet of ships was sailing toward North America. Washington decided to plan a combined French and colonial attack against the British forces in Yorktown.

This attack trapped the British Army. They could not receive supplies by sea because of the French fleet. French and colonial troops prevented the British from retreating by land.

On October 17, 1781, Cornwallis surrendered. King George did not want Yorktown to be the last battle of the war. But Parliament decided the loss was too costly. U.S. and British leaders signed the Treaty of Paris on September 3, 1783. This agreement officially ended the war.

General Washington forced the British Army to surrender at Yorktown.

A New Nation

On May 25, 1787, U.S. leaders gathered in Philadelphia to form a new government. This meeting began the system of government that the United States still uses today.

By September 1788, the U.S. Constitution was officially approved by all the states. Congress then elected George Washington the first president of the United States.

During a protest, several colonists are killed by British soldiers. This event becomes known as the Boston Massacre.

French and Indian War (1754–1763) begins.

British Parliament passes Intolerable and Quartering Acts. First Continental Congress meets and sends Declaration of Rights to King George III.

British Parliament passes Stamp Act.

1754	1765	1770	1774
1763	1767	1773	

British Parliament passes Townshend Acts.

King George passes Proclamation of 1763 after Pontiac's Rebellion.

Samuel Adams helps organize tea merchants. They protest British taxes on tea with the Boston Tea Party.

March—Patriot forces capture Dorchester Heights.

July—Congress approves Declaration of Independence.

August—Battle of Long Island occurs.

December—Battle of Trenton takes place.

September—Treaty of Paris is signed.

February—France joins forces with colonists in the war against Great Britain.

June—Battle of Monmouth occurs.

1775	1776	1777	1778	1781	1783	1788

April—Battles of Lexington and Concord signal the start of the war.

May—Second Continental Congress meets.

June—Battle of Bunker Hill occurs.

October—Battle of Saratoga takes place.

March—Battle of Guilford takes place.

October—Cornwallis surrenders after Battle of Yorktown.

George Washington is elected as the first president of the United States.

Words to Know

bayonet (BAY-uh-net)—a long metal blade attached to the end of a musket

boycott (BOI-cott)—to refuse to buy something as a way of making a protest

loyalist (LOI-uhl-ist)—a person loyal to Great Britain during the Revolutionary War

militia (muh-LISH-uh)—the military force of each colony

minuteman (MIN-it-man)—a volunteer soldier in the Revolutionary War who was prepared to fight at a minute's notice

musket (MUHSS-kit)—a gun commonly used in the Revolutionary War

patriot (PAY-tree-uht)—a person who wanted independence from Great Britain

retreat (ri-TREET)—to withdraw or move back during battle

To Learn More

Gay, Kathlyn and Martin Gay. *Revolutionary War*. Voices from the Past. New York: Twenty-First Century Books, 1995.

Kent, Deborah. *The American Revolution: "Give Me Liberty, or Give Me Death."* American War. Hillside, N.J.: Enslow Publishers, 1994.

Moore, Kay. *If You Lived at the Time of the American Revolution.* New York: Scholastic, 1997.

Useful Addresses

Adams National Historic Site
135 Adams Street
Quincy, MA 02169

Colonial National Historical Park
P.O. Box 210
Yorktown, VA 23690-0210

Independence National Historical Park
313 Walnut Street
Philadelphia, PA 19106

Jamestown-Yorktown Foundation
P.O. Box 1607
Williamsburg, VA 23187

Internet Sites

Colonial Williamsburg
http://www.history.org

**Jamestown Settlement and Yorktown Victory
    Center**
http://www.historyisfun.org

Liberty! The American Revolution
http://www.pbs.org/ktca/liberty

**The Revolutionary War: A Journey Toward
    Freedom**
http://library.thinkquest.org/10966

Index